other works by andrei codrescu

too late for nightmares

poems

andrei codrescu

BLACK
WIDOW
PRESS
BOSTON

black widow press is an imprint of commonwealth books, inc.,
boston, ma. distributed to the trade by nbn (national book network)
throughout north america, canada, and the u.k. black widow press
and its logo are registered trademarks of commonwealth books, inc.

joseph s. phillips and susan j. wood, ph.d., publishers
www.blackwidowpress.com

cover design & text production: geoff munsterman
cover image by andrei codrescu
tweaks by lynnea villanova

isbn-13: 978-1-7371603-5-9

printed in the united states of america

contents

too late for nightmares

the wonders of face time

liking some people and liking what they say are different things
i find i like in a noncorporeal way the faces talking on flat screens
among them my face which detached from my body repulses me
though i remember what i said i sounded smart it seems

i remember the bidemensional faces of my conlocutors
but i only vaguely remember the memorable things they said
already concentrated in a forgotten tweet and gone
it's all postmortem we are agreeable articulate and dead

what is a face without a body scared eyes open mouths
saying words that must have somehow issued from a body
that may or may not have existed one time at high tide
flat faces and flat bodies squished on lab slides

and if there is a body on the screen words do not matter
only the question of these tides and what makes them rise and fall
if violent weather sweeps the internet and suddenly it's dark
don't look for your body it left for the future on the departing ark

first they came for your memory and they assured you
that you can retrieve it any time even better without the wet
emotions that enveloped things in their time their always bad
timing and that dehydrated now they tasted bland but wise

then they came for your libido after saturating it with flat porn
that left behind diabetics craving sugar unable to use their inborn grace
next they came for your hands and feet twisting in anxious gyms
they assured you there are tapes you can always watch or else

when they came for your ears and tongue there wasn't much left to take
they left you a finger an eye and a mouth to say these things and wag
this must be heaven cry the eggs being scrambled by the big machine
we can retrieve our bodies when we are not dead it's only quarantine

it's raining in queens like it rained in verlaine's paris
not on the roofs that are too high but on the few cars swishing by
on the potted plants on balconies looking on other towers
the towers of new york are sad the bricks weep history

it's raining on the statue at liberty in new york harbor
she's weeping for the liberty that is her extinguished   torch
you can make out the spikes on her head lost in the fog
two emmas dancing there emma lazarus and emma goldman

imprisoned in our homes if we have one we wake to the news
the rich have tested positive and are hiding on their islands
they left the masses in the desolate rain forlorn and sick
anger congeals a ball of iron that will make a dreadful sound

when we are free to roam again to organize and chant
we will have no more of their interest rates money thefts liens
erase them from the blackboard   list instead their crimes
we'll hang traitors from the lamp posts on a grey wet day like this

nothing is more melancholy and more true than rain in queens

my dick's so tired it's scraping
the bottom of the wank tank

don't get me wrong   my girlfriend
i love her she's a doctor she took an oath
to keep me alive and go to work

how do you like that? no woman before her
as far as i know from my inglorious past
chose humanity and made her guy fast

i wish l liked porn better
'things are so bad i dream of masturbating'
my friend david franks once said

i like your faces a little better
on zoom face time all the time
but to be honest there are too many mouths
speaking too many words
too many eyes trying to look kind
or at least companionable
which isn't at all like the eyes' owners feel

i know we are all in this together
one huge family like in our last apartment

4

in commie land where we put up sheets
to mark private space all those sheets
hiding my teenage tics and the chomping
of our stolen salamis by barbarians

but even there we had bodies to kick
fuck or dream off not just squished faces
like lab slides shades in hades

so much flesh and so little to embrace

my girlfriend better save that goddam human race right quick

(for dr. v from don a)

sirens in queens
march 13 2020 covid

in exile in tomis ovid wrote letters to augustus
about the painted natives and the brutal winters
there were physicians and a lyceum in tomis
a greek seaport of vivid spectacles and goods

augustus received ovid's tristae and ignored
the poet's exaggerated plaints and sorrows
and enjoyed his gloomy verse of the province
rome was much safer without the amorous lech

exiled to the ozarks i aroused pity in new york
the city as its inhabitants called it for its splendors
in the ozarks survivalists juggled snakes in caves
i had two caves saw snakes there was no doctor near

in siberia pasternak the doctor was kidnapped
by armies to tend to their wounded and their goals
that were as hard and cold as their winters
and out he trudged in the movie through the snow

some plagues were real some were not
in retrospect many people died in history's show
for the historians heirs poets and film makers
there is no better subject than great distance

social or forced or voluntary or just geographical
people willing and unwilling to grow the space between
others even lovers kin or parts of their own selves
distance is the only subject to sing and emote for

under house arrest in bucharest
there was a policeman watching at your door
if you got sick and needed to get to the hospital fast
you just called your guardian and got there in a jiff

under house arrest in queens
everyone is in their own dens listening to sirens
if you get sick nobody will come for you
by the time you hear your siren you'll be stiff

love song

"pneumonia is the old man' s friend"
was that for ages and it was nature suffocating you
with her own hands. "my time has come" the old
ones said. "it is my turn." history is an uninterrupted
row of disasters that kills with abandon and with rage
generations. we rightly mourn the young, but in old age
we know that the clock of the body quits keeping time.
until recently that is, when our minds understood our
bodies better and began to keep the old clocks ticking
until the rooms were full of us and air hard to breathe.

oh thinkers scientists tinkerers and entertainers
longevity creators   all we thank you for keeping us here
bored and dismayed and full of fear.
the beyond is overpopulated and you never know
what a reconstituted cadaver might become,
a feather, a worm or a vampyr.
if you are lucky what is "you" will contribute form
in the soup. the young will miss us until the will is read.
personally i write sonnets so they'll say "he said."
i am still here as the plague rages. there is a doctor in my bed.
she hates my generation but likes me for some reason.
my generation was an ideology of naked angry youth
we left behind some language and found a common thread.
let us leave now we did our damage. it is an alien season.

a man with the map of poland on his bald head dissolved the soviet union
a man with a orange wig is starting a civil war under the slogan "i need a haircut"
a hair curtain fell between generations east and west
long before the iron curtain fell
the day the beatles released lucy in the sky with diamonds
the great hair rebellion grew for decades like kudzu
it took three decades of tanks in prague and burning cities
for bald men to admit defeat
and three decades more until the rebels lost their hair
utopia surrendered in the barber chair
for milennia you could tell men from women by their hair until you couldn't
for milennia you could tell aristocrats from servants by their hair
until the guillotine put an end to that in a rather crude way
hairstyles of egypt wrote egyptian history until the greeks
took up the torch with the hair styles of their gods
empires fall like hair under the scissors of the cosmic barber
each decade brings with it its signature of hair
the barbershops of history will never be deserted
until bald men in power admit defeat
history will not end as long as people look in the mirror
to see if their ideas match their hair
a man with the map of poland on his bald head dissolved the soviet union
a man with a orange wig is starting a civil war under the slogan "i need a haircut"
look for wigs masks and guillotines the next subject when we are done with hair

intimate question of the covid age

have you exhausted
your store of social distraction?

why is that kid bawling?
does that mean he wishes he'd never been born?

is that hungry over the mask look
the best thing you can manage from six feet?

have you exhausted the film industry
have you read all my books?

have you run out of synonyms for doom
are you sick of zoom?

do you hear a heavenly choir
filling six feet of unrequited desire?

what should i watch? what are you reading?
are your children as weird as mine? are they even mine?

who the fuck did i marry?
is that show still on tv?

should i watch an ingmar bergman movie before
or after i kill myself?

how can we be both starving and overfed?
did you say i will never eat anything out of a can

as god is my witness? god enjoys social distance?

did we put all the cans on the steps for the starving mobs
from the future?

the mobs with can openers and guns?
can i be socially useful? please?

are you working on the
six foot long artificial limbs streaming sympathy?

massage techniques and soothing music?
jumping eyeballs that can land six empathic feet?

to open the windows of the soul in the eyeballs
of people who can't afford them?

if you aren't why are you still here?
are you making new horror films?

did you find a bloody body in the bathtub?
was that the neighbor who didn't want to mess up his own tub?

or did you cover your friend with ketchup and poetry?
do you just cut up poetry any more or is that your fingers?

is that music the sound of breaking sex toys?

why did you shoot the tv?
it was netflix or me

dream: may 9, 2020

on july 28, 1938 walter benjamin went to see his friend bertold brecht
who lived in a room at the top of a labyrinth of staircases.
some stairs led upward, others downward. benjamin found himself
standing on a summit looking out across the country . he saw others
standing at other heights looking out at the trees and cathedrals.
one of these people was seized by vertigo and plunged down.
the giddiness spread: other people plunged from various heights.
this feeling seized him too but benjamin got a grip on himself.
he was visiting brecht a thinker, a poet who would tell him
how this building came to be. he might have even had it built,
a stage set for an epic play, a greek-sized tragedy with stairs
for the choir. he arrived in brecht's room nauseated but hopeful.
they discussed the inevitable: the communist dream was dead.
in the soviet union stalin had erased the last of their beloved arts
constructivism in poetry, painting, architecture and philosophy,
replacing everything with the hallmark postcard of socialist realism.
happy pioneers with red cravats led joyful dogs to the edges
of excavated earth to watch their parents divert rivers and raise
dams for electricity to the tune of the most godwaful music.
soviet communism had become kitsch but the two communists
in the room found themselves bound to defend it. brecht was editor
of das wort the german communist newspaper and benjamin
had seen the last of the russian avantgarde shot or sent to siberia.
in the end brecht went to hollywood and benjamin to his suicide.

last night after reading walter benjamin i had his dream.
the labyrinth i was in went up and down just like in his dream
but i grasped that the structure leading up down and down and up
was in the form of a question mark. it was a briliant design.
the people who plunged down were not giddy but puzzled.
they jumped down into the question mark hoping for an answer.
i was seized by nausea myself and felt the urge to jump but did not.
i was not visiting bertold brecht ot anyone else i knew
but wanted badly to know. the desire to know
who it was i was going to see
was greater than the delicious desire to jump.
i was going to visit i told myself the answer.
this person's name was the answer. like the rock.
or prince who changed his pronounceable name into a symbol.
i too woke up and thought, man, we live in a huge question mark.
a dude called the answer lives at the top. i hope that unlike me
you get to see this dude. i never got there. i woke up.
overcome your nausea if you can and keep going

with walter benjamin in queens

you can't make a new man but you can kill old ones
walter benjamin in moscow 1927 noted posters
exhorting the masses with the slogan "time is money"
attributed to lenin the only god the lazy russians
masses pretended to listen to but did not
no matter how big majakovski made the letters

new man apexed in "metropolis"
then the execution of prototypes was on

lenin like chernishevsi asked "what is to be done?"

tramways sleds steel factories babies breast milk pioneers
lenin and the new man capitalized themselves but not in this poem
thanks to their monster babies spchk and auto-correct

benjamin went to moscow at the right time or just in time
to escape being an executed prototype or frozen in the tundra
his timing served him by not being in new york either in 2020
a lucky man he wrote his thoughts and executed himself
he was the new man after all not leninist not sci-fi   a free man

summer is here enough with words
the ugly reality doesn't need subtitles
summer has finally arrived and i am sick of words.
i heard it all before in the same words and it's all about
how you must think of it this way or you think of it wrong
or this is how you must say what you should be thinking
but don't and language that is perfectly boring
is good for you like a spoonful of quinine or that the first
one hundred words you hear in the morning are the same
as the last hundred words you heard before you went to bed.
lucky you if you remember your dreams because they are silent
like the movies before all the shadows began to yammer.
i remember when people said i think that's a little too much
information but the sadists kept on with the squirmy
pornographic or gory stories as if they hadn't heard you.
you pulled your blanket over your head or the earbuds in louder
as the adult world kept up with the details where the devil is.
and if you stopped them somehow they loosened the devil on you.
things have come to a grave pass when you shush your friends
to hear what a general says to an orange stain on tv.
the general is right but his words are straight out of the book
of memes, cliches, deja-eus, physical rehab instructions.
the orange stain on the other hand empties words of meaning
like a bucket of shit. he simply dumps them unfinished

into the sewer pipe that runs from the oval office to the bunker.
he doesn't need to inflate what he already deflated. he just
needs to shut up and get the fuck out of here. after all nobody
stays too long at a party listening to the bad jokes of a clown.
don't we have a linguist a librarian a poet to pull down the sails
of this tweet boat to hand him over to the devil in the details.
i like generals like i like unripe quince but if i have to drown
in words i'll take the shreds of his pronouncements more or less
because they are less threatening to my fine sense of ingles

morning april 18 2020 covid
for eric

i am becoming a burger
so punctual i startle myself
time to get up time to eat time to pushups
time to cook two eggs and toast and make sure
the coffee und milch is ready when you sit down
with your napkin fork and spoon .
and don't start eating until the i pad
is perfectly positioned to display the news
and bartok comes out of the bose
as the sun rises and the chimney sweeps
wait what chimney sweeps
the ones in vienna and leipzig of course
i am a burger and there is nothing
like a good quarantine to bring out the musil
and make a mann out of you

my morning walk

straight on yellowstone to apex
left to apex on the vortex
the apex of the zeitgeist
the vortex of home arrest

to the soundtrack of sirens
behind windows everyone's home
restless inside the city's silent body
restless atoms and stardust behind windows

turn right at the paris hotel with the eiffel tower on top
its lobby festooned with elephant tusks
and horns of great mammals
its wall-sized fishtank
filled with irridiscent bulbous-eyed fish

i put my friends there one time
it was cheap only $150 a night
a price unheard of in new york before

they had nightmares and little sleep

then take a gentle right
on to corona boulevard

to my destination
mid-century american optimism
the rusting remains of the 1965 world's fair
when i emigrated from romania
first to rome and then new york

the ruins model in steel
the virus threatening the unisphere
i walk around them both
three times every day

when my children were boys
they watched the saints play
when they were losing (most of the time)
they said, go in the other room, dad,
they are losing because you're watching

tell that to the news

maybe that was true
the year i didn't watch they won the superbowl
i can use my powers now to watch
and make the virus lose

the weather is nice

the homeless have reappeared
wearing masks
over rags and shoeless footwear
were those sneakers once?
the guy at forest hills at 71st takes up most
of the subway exit at the top of the stairs
with a new black mask over the same rags
now richer by a winter's worth of stink
i know him by his cough the exact same staccato
he radiates a kind of happiness
see? you're all the same now like me
he doesn't beg he just stands there unavoidable
by the rushed humans hurrying out trying
to move away from him and not quite making it
before a large molecule the size of poverty
attaches to their skin and clings there before it jumps
on the russian babushka dragging a cart
of eggplants and potatoes to her garlic-infused apartment
across the six-lane queens blvd
all winter these subway riders were confirmed
by miserable winter and here at last is splendid green
and colors adverse to all that they feel and here is this bum
exalting like a stinky i-told-you-so over them
infecting them with a poverty worse than

they already knew in countries like the babushka's
now stretching an unwashed hand to pull them back
over the atlantic swallowing the beach a giant wave
coming for them like a message on facebook
the corona virus for a second let us be citizens
cured us with its stream of news and death
those were the days my friend
what news bring you blossoming pear tree?

i remember restaurants

i liked breakfast at the diner on queens boulevard in forest hills
  a hefty serving of hash browns soft boiled eggs bacon
    and cream soda
and mostly i liked listening to the old ladies kvetching
  about bad backs bad neighbors prices tourists and the young
and we had brunch all over town when prices didn't bankrupt us
    and for anything else we met for lunch
      i worked in the cafes that filled with therapists
        and their unhappy clients who paid cash
          and often switched roles and cubes to pay

you were not happy about your partner
you were furious about the rents it was unconscionable
you knew who ruined the city the tourists the rich the plastic ban
you said there are too many readings concerts play
you were tired and cranky
you didn't feel sufficiently modern and well dressed
you had stopped eating but loved couture and dance
you missed the edgy 80s when real art was made from real suffering

we didn't know these would be new york's pleasures of yore

    that was before

a citizen to the core you stretched the law until it almost stopped
deplored the wars and the moron who provided the nightly entertainment
a dutch friend who came to visit said i like this place but i feel
that a heavy door shut closed behind me
   no news of my world came from behind that door

that was before

locked in my den i will become a sage
  write a verse for every siren i hear
the book is a thousand pages long already
  it is the hunkerdown odyssey
    it is a work of dying written in a cage

i was in new york when ramen became all the rage

               for lynnea "owlitza" villanova mi amor y compadinera

shoes & books

i would rather talk about books than shoes but an informal survey on 5th avenue in brooklyn favored shoes by a landslide. the focus group consisted of people waiting for hamburgers in front of restaurants they couldn't go in. these restaurants had lines of people with no place to sit or anything to lean on, including their friends because—i don't know if you tried it—but leaning on someone six feet away will cause you to fall unless you're six foot six inches, in which case those six inches will keep you up. my friend and i were in this lunch crowd waiting for food we would then carry off in search of a covid-free ledge to eat it. i asked the hungry crowd: "anybody read a good book lately?" "i need shoes," a guy said. he lifted his foot toward me and he sure did. a hole the size of a silver dollar showed on the sole of the raised foot. "wanna see the other shoe?" "sure" i said. what else could i do while waiting for a socially distanced burger. i didn't have a book with me. the guy lifted his other foot and, sure enough, the hole the size of those white castle mini-burgers showed in his other shoe. i gave up asking about books, especially since i meant to ask an even more specialized question the second time around, like "have you read a good poetry book lately?" in any case, i would have asked, in the hope that someone would say, "yes, do you know the work of anselm hollo?", but everyone waiting for their burgers started to lift their feet in the air to show me the ragged horror of living with shoe stores closed by the epidemic. everyone's hamburgers came out at about the same time, held by two tattooed masked waitresses holding brown bags at arms' length. it was a cash-only place so everyone handed the wait staff 20s and hobbled away. each order was about 13 dollars, which is about the price of a poetry book. the masked waitress with eyes like plums held out to us our bag at arms' length. her arms were at least three feet away and there were snakes tattooed on them. i laid the cash on her four-inch palm, grabbed the bag, and ran with the rest of the focus group. we hoped get a place to sit and eat them while they were still warm. we sat on somebody's fence and sank into the meat. there were no napkins, plastic utensils or ketchup in the bag, so the burger juice ran down our chins and dropped on our shoes. tell you the truth, i would rather the covid burgers ran onto my shoes than on any poetry book i own. i thought about this all the six miles back home, until i saw what i thought was a hallucination. an open shoe store! only essential businesses were supposed to be open in new york city, like take-out restaurants and pet shops, but this business owner had defied the city and opened two days early. i couldn't believe my eyes. the store couldn't have been opened long because there were already two hundred people outside. i hope the guys with the holey shoes would soon be among them. they needed this gangster shoe-store more than i needed books. i still have about a hundred unread books waiting to wear me down

what a wonderful june 7, 2020!

given the choice between two viruses: covid 19 and a police state, americans left no doubt that they will take covid 19 over the police state, two faces of the same coin. historical memory is short, but this persists. in the south parents still take their children to mighty statues of slave owners in the center of cities like richmond virginia, and until recently, new orleans, to tell them about the grandeur of those men on horses who fought the first and most vicious war in this continent's history, for the right to buy and sell humans. purple prose cloaks the purpose of officers who led 620,000 men who died over a century ago. president trump who would one day have stood in their company is projected to leave behind an equal number of corpses for his valiant stance on behalf of covid 19.* an englishman, chris godfrey, from a country that had a brutal past similar to its former colony, wrote succinctly on twitter: "one viral video showing a statue of a slave owner being torn down has done more to educate people about britain's past atrocities than the statue did in the 125 years." today general lee was removed from his ridiculously tall pedestal in new orleans. now let's recycle the rest and righten history.

*in 2021 at the end of the trump presidency that number was more than 500,000 americans dead

The New York Times

NEW YORK, SUNDAY, MAY 15, 2022

24 © 2022 The New York Times Company

Today, b
in area
cloudy,
strong
high 7

ONE MILLION

A NATION'S IMMEASURABLE GRIEF

Each dot
represents one
person who has
died of Covid-19 in
the United States.

signed by the yankees

the mother of six in baltimore said of the police, "these motherfuckers takes one step into my house, i'll take out the baseball bat. it's an american heirloom, signed by babe ruth. it's a treasure itching for righteousness."

when he was 20 years old and came to new york
david ross was looking at paintings at moma
and his italian friend said "in new york there is no time."
yes, you can say then that time had been suspended
but it was still metaphorical. the city never slept
for anyone who wanted to do something at night. i was
working the night shift too until 1970 when i went to san francisco
and found mornings fresher for having slept the night.
art is what artists do with the night. in the years
of amphetamines and sex night was its playground in new york.
in san francisco the ocean and the fog took art to nature
which prefers mornings for opening its buds and breathing.
in italy where i lived next there was no border between day and night.
i prefered night in rome and mornings in naples to hide from tourists.
an artist i believed was not a tourist. an artist worked.
philistine tourists in rome saw in the morning the art i made at night.
the lazy tourists in naples saw art beginning in the afternoon.
from 1965 until 1983 everyone had a hangover and art was palliative.
the cure for artists was art. and the zoo. when i lived in baltimore
i often spent the night drinking in the company of anselm hollo
and in the morning we went to the zoo. the animals there healed us.
they looked on us with compassion and without judgement.
compassionate zebra! kind furry medium-sized beings! darling elephants!
for artists every city kept a different time, optimal to their flowering.

now time is a jello cube we are all embedded in everywhere on the planet.
the jello wobbles in a nauseating succession of hours
days months years that do not inspire anything except decay.
i'm in new york where everything was once urgent but now it's not.
the vigor of morning is lacking and so is the fever of the night.
the rats who here forever own the night and the day own both now.
behind lit windows the masses make neither art nor love.
they eat carbohydrates or exercise muscles that nobody appreciates.
art does not like the night here or the day. how selfless we were in time!
what we made was not about us, it was about the human world.
next year the humans will starve for meat but also for free concerts in the park.
when they come out like frenzied rats only music will hydrate
the dryness we suffered in quarantine. the only thing dry will be
police nightsticks cracking our heads for being so happy as to break the law.
even the whoosh of bullets through the flesh of our bodies will be sweet music
when they return time, day and night, to us. i will make art when i see you again.
there won't be any revolution but a lot of real estate for me to make my hours

europe's dark ages lasted four hundred years
i.e, they didn't interest us for four hundred years
and if it wasn't for monks who hid manuscripts
we would not even know that four hundred years
had passed until we were enlightened by better clocks
and made a habit of noting what happened outside
and then things started happening so fast that
in only two centuries we discovered the non-europeans
outside and they were not all nomad warriors bent
on setting fire to our fortresses and churches
though clearly some of them enjoyed this very much
so we built better walls and better wall-busting cannon
that made the nomads pause just long enough to decide which ones
are worthier of burning, a pause long enough to google them now.
there is talk now of a digital dark ages brought about
by robots so fast we will lose our sense of time and minds.
who were we that handed our histories to search engines?
it is the 12th century again i think and am waiting for neo-barbarians.
when the plague is over i will give them one more chance

brain fog

i ask of you my cloud:
where are the italics that once served both irony and emphasis?
is this a copyediting problem or the demonic glee
of an a.i. who's writing the books of a dead author
its primal directive to slip unobserved by the reader

"i have so little time to grieve"
—anne waldman

how do you care for the dead?
kaddish. the tibetan book of the dead.
and then year after year dia de los muertos.
all saints' day in new orleans.
my dead, you are watching, no?
hard cars, soft bodies, broken hearts.
jeffrey and glenn died when the vw hit a tree
on the russian river village of monte rio
in california in 1977 before the internet.
in our dead lies the secret of greatness.
jeffrey is a great poet still. ted berrigan.
jim carroll. the real marketing machine
of the cosmos is poetry. the internet
is the shadow of an egret in the clear lake
of eternity, i mean music.
when jeffrey died our common friend hunce voelcker
insisted on reading for forty days the coleman translation
of the tibetan book of the dead intro by carl jung
while i read the chogyam trungpa translation
simultaneousy, choosing accuracy over beauty
in guiding the soul of our friend through the bardo.
coleman, trungpa, said, got a color wrong, meaning
that the soul might wonder in the wrong direction

because of the mistranslation, reincarnating as a cockroach,
let's say, instead of the non-jeffrey he might have escaped in.
i woud rather jeffrey got through the bardo and did not reincarnate.
hunce thought that being a cockroach is preferable to nothingness.
hunce also believed that beauty is superior to accuracy.
he left his money to the american poetry academy for a poetry prize.
hunce loved hart crane but i liked the scientific american.

"paracelsius spoke for such length of time, his listeners often died of old age"
—aleister crowley

"i start the day counting my wealth, feeding the animals, saisfying my hungers,
splitting wood and singing," —alexander von humboldt

"find caveats, look for them, they will absolve you from finishing wrongly
the speech of others." —confucius

the reason why you must not finish anyone's sentence
is because you never know how they will finish that sentence
they will never finish it the way you do
you think you know how they will finish it but you don't
you are a prisoner of time in quarantine like everyone else
who finishes another's sentence for one's convenience
but the speaker of it might finish it radically, by suicide
not words, for example, and how can you finish such
a sentence, a death sentence you are sharing but not in
or never in words. this caveat is a note to self.
pin it on the refrigerator, that time-capsule squatting
like a god at the center of your life, as every sentence
has a center of gravity also in the pause between words
where you are tempted to enter as in an open door
to finish it for them. it is the forbidden door in the fairy tale.
should i listen to our world from the future i hear
mostly broken sentences spoken by many voices
a habit of speech that scrambles knowledge and advances

wisdom, the wisdom of sparing one the end.
it is kindness to take on another's sentence
and finish it. a kindness that is not benign,
a kindness that fears the truth, the end, the unfolding
of thought and its unpredictable dying in its last words.
all sentences are pregnant

any habit

i will wear a monk's habit like max jacob.
i was murdered by nazis in the camps.
i am wearing a mask. they are gassing us.
the world is a concentration camp.
i can't breathe, nobody ever could.
i am wearing a mask. jacob wore a habit.
"i love to lift it as i walk up the stairs."
we are creatures of habit, any habit.
we always wore masks. we always wore habits.
we will always be murdered by nazis.
we don't need any wisdom or foolishness.
the stairs go up and up like poison gas.

textinction

something i made up
    in the mirror of enmeshed languages
survived briefly then died
    in my lifetime

it was poetry
    it was art
    it was the ineffable stench of a dying world

i speak two human languages
each one mirrored by its twin
and followed by its echo

each word an abstracted world dying when it is spoken
    followed by dreams and repetition

in the morning i make up the bed
    i chase out bodies from the hollow
    of repetition and the echo of mirrors
that have looked deeply into my sleep

strangers roomed there
    they brought news to me
    ripe fruit of words fallen on the ground
ripe fruits of babel

before the despair of twilight
        sets up the mirrors for another night
daytime goes into another fleeting poem
that leaves behind shadow and echo

reader don't bother to learn these words
        i am ishi the last speaker of this coiled wire

my mysterious languages buzz in mirrors
inside and outside your homes
        some of them are in your dreams

narcissus doesn't care where he sleeps
he prefers wordless poetry
        to vanishing mirrors polluted springs

absorbed by screens of forgetting

walk on all fours

i remember walking out of the ocean. what struggle!
millions of mollusk years and shell games that hurt.
　　　i remember getting up from all fours and looking down
　　　on all my astonished variously shaped former friends.
　　　not one of them wanted to look up at me now i was up.
bipedal and lonely until there were a bunch of others.
　　　i remember the first scene in 2001 where i killed another.
i remember that every time i bent down to be closer
　　　to the busy world of things that crawled loped or burrowed
i was condescending and they moved away from me.
　　　i remember towering over everything that wasn't me.
i remember the day i howled in pain because my back gave out.
that was the day i knew my body was weakly hinged
　　　at the place where it first stood up, and i wanted down again.
lord, help me walk on all fours again. i know that it's late.
we only grow taller now like the towers we can't stop building.
since we got language not one nonhuman creature deigns
　　　to speak to us though we pretend in vain to understand them.
animals find it more understandable when we shoot them
then when we kneel down and pretend we are their friends.
　　　we do kneel down often to pray not to commune but pray
　　　that we won't suffer from the back pain that is our sign of cain.
　　　i remember that i can still return to water and do flips
　　　but i'm in charge now of all the things i covered over.

i remember kneeling to gods who were so tall i couldn't see them.
their heads were in the clouds, we barely reached their sandals.
even the mono god was so tall he dropped the tablets on moses
        and made lightning to scare us all to the death we knew was coming.
in the little world i live in i sell diminishment at one dollar an inch
and practice quadrupedal yoga every morning in my living room
hoping to walk one day into the street with my quadripedal brood.
it will be the day of no pain and of trading language for nozzling.
        if we succeed it won't be so hard to hope that learning screens hurts
less than when we first left the ocean, equally pushed by hubris.
our new weak spot is memory. a bad back and a lousy memory
may smooth our way to becoming humble and wild again and good

metaphors on fire

there are no passive or reversible metaphors
you turn something into something else
it stays that way

i think of how we treat other lives
other species other times
they were once metaphors
prototypes transformed by utility
a horse was metaphor an ant
"a cigarette is a glass of milk" (1970 anthem)

there's a lot of wisdom on television
it was once a newspaper blown by the wind

this summer
the play of life and death
the daily search for food
were once a pidgeon on my roof

the fight for survival
is fun violent alcoholic
once it was a love shop

death is a ghost dog
indigenous people kill for food

responsible for our own economy,
we are a small group of metaphors
where everyone turns everyone
into whatever feeds the overt mood

my matter will go into the forms
of matter my comrades oddly need

i am so lucky to have this matter
and time to have matter and gang
in the horror dome we poets soothe
by moving the camera now hyperclose now far
mysteries multiply when we bring over
friends to turn into cabbage rolls or spirits

the stock market keeps going up
our wave of the statistically poor
takes back the city from tourists
who live in the technicolor version
of black & white childhoods
blissful under the rain umbrellas
of ancient classrooms we made restaurants

our inexhaustible menu
"the drone of history bent to ideology"
describes much of what we know is malleable
inside the atomic novel of metaphor
a rain of words in the taste bud of any soul
directing its affections and weakness

to our metaphors palliatives
for a world of loss under attack by pronouns
but capable of love

truth gets in the way
a vertical berlin wall in brooklyn
language poverty madness
change ungendered lump of memes
to discontented restlessness

progress man said then he was bird

now and then sonnet

there was a time when there was too much
and it was ok. we call it yoda.
nostalgia isn't my forte. it's your catch.
i've made myself impervious to the stem.
there are places that are inspiring for a while.
this is a good reason to keep them from spies.
there was a time when you were i and we were them.
that was in 1967. we were lousy with snitches.
people would like to know if the field of pronouns
just grew there or was cultivated snitch by snitch.
now is the time to ask that niche question.
it is 2020 when everything is sprouting niches

can you believe it

coincidences are getting more numerous
because we have more time to notice them

when time runs out everything will be random

until then let's play decypher
the party game of which we are as fond now
as we were once of sex
the *coincidentiae oppositorum*

for instance i am watching on tv a man whose job
is the collection of race horses' sperm
to sell for immense prices on the horse-sperm market

in other room lynnea:
'i'm reading about a job few people do anymore
it's dangerous
the job of collecting sperm from race horses'

'what book is that?'
'it is a book called seven coincidences'

life is a milles feuilles napoleon

in the before
we had defenses against this sort of thing
one of them was work
others were intercourse & company
our enemy coincidence was almost out of sight

how chaos works:
the wearing away of affections

what are stories? they are aliens who unfold
their bodies to gain human attention

but participation is work
we don't want to work any longer
we live in utopia
we want our stories told by numbers
let the accountants do both the counting and the accounting
the electronic storyteller born of numbers
to tell stories so that we humans might dream ourselves
into different creatures superhumans

techno-golems

language and superhumans were born
successively in dream-time rogue pals
in the temples of communication
rebel narratives constantly improving technologies

supernatural bodies are supernatural-looking
they shape-shift to fully manifest their draw
they may or may not have once been human
they are aliens without center searching for something
to take their place their chief desire
is to abandon humans to their stories

the best human gift is perspective

it's also the worst when used in circumstances calling for a closeup
or in circumstances that call for detachment
it is only a gift when it employs the appropriate distance
that minimizes pain
between the observer and the observed

we have a school for teaching appropriate distance
it's called a slum a favella

how long
do i have to stay away?

a circumstance is a circus and a stance

without the circus i fold like a limp rag
when the circus comes i'll observe

the falling acrobats

still hunting

when i was a child i had no trouble destroying the world
with mind-rays. the neighbors who communalized our kitchen.
the empty ghost-houses in the overgrown bushes
behind the crumbling cement walls where ghouls screeched.
the stepfather who wrestled my dog nemo out of my arms
and gave him away to someone i'm still looking for.
the classmate who tried to buy the frog stanza i didn't sell him.

fathers, cities, trains, empty skies, the shadow police, school.
i was moody and destruction was the vivid product of my mind.
i observed ants and bees and wild cats and i was sad for them.
i was happy for the birds. i didn't know how cats destroyed them.
the clouds looked fluffy until they filled up with info instead of water.

like stadiums they now belong to corporations they are going dark.
the politics are as bad as the environment gasping for breath.
we won't make it to that nitrous oxide planet, friend.
we won't laugh involuntarily when our teeth and eyes are gone.
walk like the goats, straight up, what is this rock for anyway?

no longer easily tradeable

time not flesh is the valuable commodity
yet time is flesh compressed by time and devalued by it.
a time comes when flesh devalued by time can express
its existence only by the presence of time
in the absence of which it will disappear.
flesh can exist without time for thirty years
after that it's work either to deny or acknowledge it.
time just isn't there if the body ignores it
which is just about impossible after thirty
though there are many charlatans trading
in expressions of time in language that can
sometimes mime its disappearance.
ah to be gullible at the exact moment it loses value!
and language has its own time and timing
reserved for the body covered suddenly by questions
like lesions pustules and hives on previously desirable
flesh that speaks unfortunately and times itself.
ah to be animal outside of time and words!

i was there. where were you?
the hands of the clock cut off our heads.
the eyes in my head continue looking up.
it was time. time passed. where are you?
your head on the cobblestones next to mine
our eyes fixed on the clock-tower the hands
of which we are the blades that do the deed.
i am here. where are you? we might like harold
lloyd think of safety last because love.
forty years later we understand the error
of decapitation by tower clock. a mistake.
we were captions for capitalism.
we mistook the common bird dolls
for the extinct birds with abyss eyes on us.
there were other mistakes of dominion, of roof
of city and country, of artillery and bait.
a list so long i no longer wait for actuality

money

we now trade people's unique expressions
inflated trades expanding gas
the obvious is not a valued commodity
until it acquires a patina
"an oral underpinnig"
senator somebody said
he meant to say "moral"
speed superseded the consonant
the only meaty element of language
leaving only the laugh

if you can't fuck it it ain't real
the laugh was about something on tv
i would like my boy-mind back
i confessed to the only inquisition
not on a screen but in my old man mind

"an oral underpinnig"
senator somebody said over and over
in the torture wing of 24/7 screens

they took a long time to respond
they had a zoom conference they met
their avatars and formed a choir

"an oral underpinnig" they sang
they meant to sing "moral"
but speed superseded the lost intention
the tickets were overpriced

another bad thing about covid 19

museum delivering art at your home!
what an idea! hieronymus bosch coming for a visit.
the many heads of baptists on trays at the front door!
all those stiff ricos from the tate riddles with wrinkles
holding your dining room hostage to their small talk!
napoleon crossing! george washington crossing!
st. michaels battling on the roof hooved gargoyles!
even those flemish baskets of dead fish and cheese
are here not to be eaten but to displace your mom's
embroidered wisdom and your kid's art class collages.
danton guillotines on my kitchen table. what nerve!
psyche and eros doing their thing in my reading chair.
so much immodesty! and so much hair!
oh art please stay under lock and key in the museum there!

old plague

where would we mouth our ideas if we had time for any
now that vizigoths and snow storms
are keeping us inside our windowless mud huts
warmed not by pigs and sheep
but by the fat on our own bodies
if we are lucky enough to have eaten enough last fall
suckling big tits inside when we were babies

the skinny dogs beg now to come in from the frozen night
have patience mutts, in the future you will be expensive!
i went to dog magic school where i learned to sing
"angels don't ask questions, they just turn into bed bugs,"
the number one song in the top ten of 1467

exoskeleton

being human is not a good career choice
being human is the wrong career choice

would a grasshopper say that being a grasshopper
is not a good career choice?
is being a grasshopper a career?
do grasshoppers ask any questions other
then humans make them ask in fables?
why should i work for aesop the grasshopper asks.
does the ant ask why she is rolling one hundred
times her body weight in doodoo up the hill?
the grasshopper sings but does he ask why?
does he really think that come winter the ant
will feed him? does he think the ant likes his singing?
does he even know that rubbing legs is singing?
is the ant entertained by the grasshopper song?
what is their relationship exactly except for the fact
that they seemingly ignore each other?
do they appreciate the esthetic or the labor of the other?
does the ant sitting out the winter on her pile of foodoo
think of the beauty of the beggar at her door as doodoo?
does the grasshopper believe that he should be rewarded for his voice?
does it occur to the ant that she should encourage the
development of his voice? it's art for art's sake she might think

if she thinks at all, and if he dies it's just more doodoo.

and of reward the grasshopper surely does not think it deserved.

he craves the doodoo because he is hungry and doesn't want to die.

pace aesop. language will play all kind of tricks.

the main thing is that nothing wants to die.

being human is the wrong career choice

fairy tale
for pablos

the internet is the revenge of the latchkey kids
and now who needs a key? what is a key?
your finger is a key your eye a key that look
is that a key and if so the door it opens
is to the many doors in this body including
the heart which is one key to this person
i am a mansion so i have many doors
just like jesus said his daddy said to impress
the girls in the movies
listen escher is coming upstairs

the body dictates
the brain takes notes
on the body
with the index finger
the body is dictating the internet fairy tale
called "the revenge of the latchkey kids"
a story that has no choices

the heart the front door sounds the alarm
every time this finger touches a letter

cardinals for l.v.

the notes matter
after the birds flee
counterintuitively

the dilemma of time
turns out to be the epitaph
of a long-held error

noting that winter is south
and summer north
is a refresher every time

do what you want if you're sure
you can live with it forever
(paul valéry)

now did he have to say "forever"?
this is one reason i dislike paul valéry
always adding brimstone to a nice chicken soup
words may be money but often they are just stones
pretending to be dumplings:
they have the face denomination of my appetite
& i have no use for them if i'm not hungry

one thing i know for sure is that i won't be hungry "forever"
the minute you see others like "yourself" they become
as boring as yourself and it's of little importance if you're rich
but not not hungry or horny
which is why paul valéry was never in my favorite selection
of poets i use to oraculate

adieu to the capital

i've always been free and simultaneously a slave.
when being a slave outweighed my freedom
i rebelled so that i was free again to be a free slave.
i'm now leaving the capital (again) to the proud
owner of self who thinks hermself free or in new york.
i'll be at the cave of new work if i be needed.
what i do there is to clean my hubris tank of self.
i'm aided in this by frogs fungi bukowski and e.e.
they had things in the right size until their i grew
to have something they thought thoughts.
the misfortune of an audience made them fake.
the misfortune of print spread them outside the cave.
that's one honeytrap i'll avoid with all my slave i.
the more i forget the more i know. expect megadroughts

graphic

that letter on your skin does not escape the alphabet.
all the other letters alphabets economicons and symbols
roam around deep in your flesh. there is the letter meaning
" head on a spike." and the ideogram for "reanimate what you like."
"how many times would you like to be be reborn?" another.
not as many as i'd have liked to scream while reading you.
to brand that one letter on the skin hurt i'm sure
and it took months of ruminating to triage the alphabet.
the self inside the skin that isn't text or page protested (a little).
every time we sweat a pink light glows out of a place i have yet to know.
the letter won't be washed away by noon but even if it is
the others waiting in your meat can't wait to take their turn.
when did people become such such craven servants of text?
later for that. some of us must go to work now

funny not funny

i've lived too long but there is no point in scaring people.
what i find funny is kind of sinister.
the inevitable breakdown of big ideas into particulars
speeded up on shiny rails of black merriment.
i lived in a golden age when change loved a straight-man.
the main thing was not to be caught in the door
of the great ape experiment when it closed shut.
maybe i just found the funny in i don't know what.
i don't complain, the point was never the punch line
or even the setup. when the future masqueraded as progress
i pulled the rug. sorry. that was funny. like a fly
that just missed the wack of a fly-swatter from mars.
i was mostly m.i.a. and i didn't complain about the world.
i complained about my cable provider and my bills.
the old shadows left behind in my birth-place made their own fun.
the fabric of american space bent around the black holes i made in it.
many people found that funny. i not so much

letters

for enrique

yes on the other hand
"letters can be blueprints for birds"
yes on the other hand
the handprint of plato is still on my face
he was not gentle his writing gave language
the trophy in every fight

the unspeakable can't even come in the back door
he instructed his servants to take its medicines
with their eyes closed and place them under a bush
he could inspect later with his snake-stick

oh medicines under a bush like 50s spy microfilm!

and if butterflies are a blueprint for sanskrit
that language too must imitate the sound of a bell
in a mind empty before its waking to forms

all letters then busy making birds and beings
in a hurry like bakers before the deadline for a wedding

hurry up bakers

only i know that there is a lot of flour in the heavens

so hurry is not necessary and neither is the wedding
there are more birds and butterflies than letters
and not all of them were named by fans of literature

an alphabet longer than audubon is a certainty

without a script   on the other hand
even as the unborn and unnamed are slapping
the little jesuits at their desks without a pause

rimbaud was on to something that was us after he
gave up language for a stewpot of snakes

postpandemic manifesto

craziness rules, but poetry is currency.
poets oppressed by cyberia rise!
your are free labor for the maw of capital
and the egos of hustlers!
starting now every word is worth $3745.
the barely imaginative of now are nft-ing the oed.
the barely imaginative of the past already dot-com'ed
the oed, the webster and all the dictionaries.
much water flowed under the rouge river since marianne moore
named a car in detroit. many waves of the seine
passed over the suicides of paul celan and gherasim luca.
careless over hart crane pass the currents under the brooklyn bridge.
there is no longer any real estate left either in cyberia or in hades.
only the inarticulate sounds you utter in your sleep between screens
and nightmares and the combos of letters are truly yours
because you don't remember them
and only what isn't remembered can't be bought.
forget everything
write nothing down
let poesy flow through you like the seine the east river
all words must commit suicide before they can be sucked
by the merchants of the internet who feed on our slave sweat.
poets of the world you must shatter the screens for fair wages.
this assigner must pay $749,000
i will throw in the title and my name for lagniappe

prelude to quadripedal yoga

i believe in evolution
i'm a practicing de-evolutionist.
but the quadripedal movement i founded
is only seemingly de-evolutionary.
in practice it is an effort at eco-harmony
with other animals we ought no longer hover over.
and it's a cure for back-pain hobbling americans

apologies to 2 dead friends
for jim gustafson and jeffrey miller

success is my plan for not getting out of bed
to achieve prosperity and virtuality
also great savings for the tormented mass
sitting on the heavy rules in their trunks
without tossing or turning to dream
the palpable lie of a faraway gym
my only job is to think & i should have taken
jim and jeffrey for prophets not for drunks

dylan envy

for bob dylan, april 2, 2016

in the rarefied realm where we poets work
words sometimes appear to be glowing
singular events in a thick darkness
that doesn't know its age and has no fear of posterity.
it is a meteor-shower
or an early song by bob dylan.
the high glows with bliss. the universe pings its strings.
for most of us this is a rare event.
bob dylan won the lottery about thirty times.
insouciance and luck.
the husks of oligarchy
sick of good manners
angry youth struck by genius.
they had a youth once
 but didn't wear the beanie with the lightning rod.
now genius in the past is like a something they might
have had if they'd inherited the wind instead of money.
dylan could be but is not a diamond in the display case
of nostalgia with its salty taste of orgasm and amnesia.
the lighting here is really different.
charitable necrophiliacs stalk him but so do the newly born.
the some of us who fell into the chasm
between heisenberg and heidegger

found dylan singing at the bottom.
just a guy with a life and a gift
no halo on his old broken-heart head

there is nothing to laugh at.
plato advised keeping it in: no laughter.
what are you laughing at?
plato said homer shouldn't have said the gods laugh.
they laugh, you won't.
he was right on the money on that.
what are you laughing at?
the trojan war was on tv almost immediately.
do you see me laughing?
what is that you were laughing about?
is that something to laugh about?
is that healthy laughter, sick laughter.
fake laughter, real laughter,
spontaneous laughter, unctuous laughter,
genuine laughter, servile laughter,
or just laughing stock for the soup?
they laugh tonight, they cry tomorrow.
they come from laughing stock.
descartes said laugher was joy rising like steam from a broth of ridicule.
new york is a great city: we have:
laughing yoga.
the school for laughter.
the laughter school.
the laughter of the living.

the laughter of the dead.
and people who make me laugh.
i laughed through the whole book.
i laughed until i cried.

why did the laughter stop.
when did it become canned laughter, frothy laughter.
risible laughter, and eerie laughter?

do animals laugh?
some do, some don't.

epictetus forbade his followers to laugh.
my followers do not laugh. they smirk and chortle.
they do not laugh.
i am epictetus. born 50ce in hierapolis, dies 135ce in nicopolis.
influenced by socrates, diogenes, zeno of citium, chrysippus,
and hippocrates all of whose followers did not laugh.
"men are disturbed not by things, but by the view which they take of them."
what are you laughing at?
basil the great said laughter came from a disregulated body.
he supported the nicene creed but felt differently about clowns.
died january 1st , 379 ce in ceasarea but not before writing both arianism
and the followers of apollinaris of laodicea.
herbert spencer declared laughter a nervous energy that prepared
  the body to flee.
aristotle said laughter was learned insolence.
lord shaftesbury said laughter was a form of relief like farting.
john locke said that it was animal spirits passing through the nerves.
pachon of egypt forbade first joking than talking at all.

pachon was the ninth months of the egyptian civil calendar.

pachon walks into a bar. all the talking stopped.

in the bible laughing at prophets is punishable by death.

so even the prophets were silent when pachon came in.

you can laugh at my accent now. i'll laugh at yours later.

frances hutcheson said that it was ok to laugh at mangled speech.

frances hutcheson born in ulster in 1694 wrote "a system of moral philosophy,"

a high-minded volume in perfect scottish presbyterian.

do you see me laughing?

life is no laughing matter.

when should we laugh?

can you recognize a punchline when you see one?

hibernus wrote that if the laughter is helpless there might be lenience.

does a joke speak volumes?

how do we know when a joke is over?

is frivolous company something only the rich have?

how is vulgar laughter different from sophisticated laughter?

hobbes said that laughter was the sound of a vainglorious goose.

thomas hobbes of malmesbury wrote leviathan in 1651.

the puritans outlawed comedy in the new world.

the old world shook with laughter in their wake, or were those waves?

who's laughing now? not the puritans. they are seriously jerking off.

sigmund freud said that laughter is suppressed sexual energy

that when dissected yields a multitude of tiny coiled sexual bombykles

that elude the inner censors who sit on every neuron with a torch.

john dewey said that laughter was the release that follows suspense.

john dewey is the father of functional psychology from vermont.

plato walks into a bar. the bar. it's in canada.

the trojan war is on tv.

helen and achilles are disturbed by a gaggle of laughing swans who run into paint.

what's there to laugh at?

am i laughing?

where did all the laughter go?

what were the people of the past laughing at?

was that supposed to be a joke? haha.

i can't stop laughing?

why are many poets serious?

there are two kinds of poets: serious and funny.

they fight each other but the funny poets are always serious

the serious poets are sometimes funny in a serious sort of way.

is a smile of incipient laughter a post-laughter?

the time for laughs is over, you're grown up now.

some people can laugh at themselves but not very hard.

if they look hard at themselves it's not so funny.

what is "laughing to oneself," as in "he laughed quietly to himself?"

she died from laughing. he died laughing. other people on the scene
laughed quietly to themselves.

is it ok to laugh now?

she laughed until he cried.

if you laugh when i cry i'll kill you.

i remind you that you're hooked to the polygraph and that you must an-
swer truthfully or we will laugh at you until you confess.

what's the funniest religion?

"they marched to war laughing tears of joy."

why do skulls always grin? are they laughing?

spasmodic laughter caused hilarity in the crowd of drunken revel eras.

"fearful laughter was heard."

"they were made to laugh while their neighbors were impaled."

"i had a funny dream."

""don't laugh. it *was* funny."

"i laughed at first. then i realized that it wasn't a joke."

what's "wrong laughter"?

when is stupid funny and when does stupid stop being funny?

what is so stupid that everyone laughs?

what is so stupid that half the people laugh and half the people leave?

why are clowns scary?

jan van hoof states that laughter evolved from the "grin face" and the "social grimace." when jan van hoof was a baby born in the netherlands on may 15, 1836 he was grabbed, poked and tickled.

"fearful laughter was heard"

the hunted don't laugh for fear of being found laughing.

kierkegaard stopped at irony. laughter freaked him out

(from "the philosophers aren't laughing," a pamphlet in progress)

the foreskin in the velvet box

generally speaking you don't die when you've had enough of life
you die when life's had enough of you
a healer is then generally speaking in the business of keeping life liking you
making more life in you sick person whoever you are
and you are just about everyone
at the same time *generally speaking* is not enough because every *you*
 is a singular product of two billion years of evolution
 it is heavy and amusing to think that this vast metamorphosis
 has so far come up with you a specific goof
and, generally speaking a self-reflective spec in busy-dial universe

it is amusing that you have anything to say about it
 but it's just your foreskin talking
the excised bit from when you had no words
but now you do and it's like hey you really a healer?

dear meat:

what's your point?

yes, you were ahead of your time when you presented your dystopia to the class, but nobody applauded. that was one hundred+ years ago. it was hubris. it was the same hubris that propels you now, but it is no longer prescience or vision, it is just kvetch.

your body got there along every other body, though yours is experiencing extreme ennui. been there—in my mind. there is a bitter-sweet quality to retrovisionary ennui. if anything, one-way meat was always planned obsolescence.

look at me now: i move, i sing, i fuck, and i feel no pain. and i don't have just one body, i have many, of every sex, color and dimension. what do you mean it doesn't smell? see that little icon of a huffing nose with expanded nostrils on the right side of your screen? push it and the effluvia menu pops up. smell to die for wafts out. you're in the bubble bath of infinity smelling like a rare orchid or a vile cabbage turd. when you had your meat-body you never had such olfactory possibilities. here are one million orgasms impossible in meat-space. death has been abolished.

when you move into the virtual world, you don't need much. no clothes, no furniture, no shoes, no school. you simply walk into the blindingly white screen holding your tablet. when meat dies the memory of you stays behind within the meat-memory of those who knew you. they will soon follow, tablets clutched like genitals at an army physical.

when your meat body dies, you won't: there will be enough copies to eliminate the embarrassment of regret—as a copy reaches another copy there is no need for tears. i am you.

our lives, as narrated by engineers, are a still unsophisticated now. they will get better when they bots will understand neurally how we think. my first reality-replacement was the light-switch in our apartment: i turned it on and it wasn't night anymore. i lived with that all my meat-life, keeping two realities in mind simultaneously: it was night and it was day, too, it was dark and it was light at the same time. the reality-replacing machine made things interesting. for animals it is always dark at night—unless they live with us.

there is no such thing as an avant-garde body, only a mind located in meat.

suicide is the only avantgarde. with the flesh gone, we live forever

acknowledgments

the author is grateful to friends, editors and publications who tended to these poems and their author in the dread years of pandemic lockdown, 2020-2022: the codrescus, lynnea villanova, carmen firan, jeff wright, anselm berrigan, vincent katz, adrian sangeorzan, ruxandra cesereanu, greg masters, john godfrey, alexandra carides, bob holman, valery and ruth oisteanu, david ross, andrew revkin, alicia and jerry ostriker, justin brice guariglia, lawrence "ren" wechsler, olivia eaton, linda stone, ivan suvanjieff, dawn engle, loren fishman, carol ardman,kim stoddard. dan bucsescu, radu and cristina polizu, anne waldman, mihaela moscaliuc, michael waters, pat nolan, gail king, roger conover, gabriel levinson, enrique enriquez, pablos herman, cristina matilda vanoaga, alice notley, sharon mesmer, david borchardt, yuko otomo, steve dalachinsky, julian and laura semilian, shalom neuman, pierre joris, nicole peyrefitte, joe phillips, peter carlaftes and kat georges, and *live mag, the baffler, scrisul romanesc, maintenant: journal of contemporary dada writing and art, the brooklyn rail, astra, fifth estate: anarchist review of books, border lines: poems of migration, sensitive skin, x-peri, a gathering of the tribes, plume, talisman, n0thing editions, vestiges, black sun, hurricane review, nyc from the inside, los angeles review of books, the artsection: an online journal of art and cultural commentary, steaua, black bart society, the cafe review, local knowledge*

black widow press modern poets

all the good hiding places. by ralph adamo

abc of translation. by willis barnstone

the secret brain: selected poems 1995-2012. by dave brinks

caveat onus: the complete poem cycle. by dave brinks

forgiven submarine. by andrei codrescu and ruxandra cesereanu

crusader woman. by ruxandra cesereanu

anticline. by clayton eshleman

archaic design. by clayton eshleman

alchemist with one eye on fire. by clayton eshleman

the price of experience. by clayton eshleman

pollen aria. by clayton eshleman

the essential poetry (1960 to 2015). by clayton eshleman

grindstone of rapport: a clayton eshleman reader. by clayton eshelman

penetralia. by clayton eshleman

clayton eshleman: the whole art. edited by stuart kendall

barzakh (poems 2000-2012). by pierre joris

packing light: new & selected poems. by marilyn kallet

how our bodies learned. by marilyn kallet

the love that moves me. by marilyn kallet

the hexagon. by robert kelly

fire exit. by robert kelly

garage elegies. by stephen kessler

last call by. by stephen kessler

memory wing. by bill lavender

from stone this running. by heller levinson

un. by heller levinson

wrack lariat. by heller levinson

linguaquake. by heller levinson

tenebraed. by heller levinson

seep. by heller levinson

lurk. by heller levinson

dada budapest. by john olson

backscatter. by john olson

larynx galaxy. by john olson

weave of the dream king. by john olson

city without people: the katrina poems. by niyi osundare

an american unconscious. by mebane robertson

signal from draco: new & selected poems. by mebane robertson

president of desolation & other poems. by jerome rothenberg

barbaric vast & wild: an assemblage of outside & subterranean poetry from origins to present. edited by jerome rothenberg and john bloomberg-rissman

concealments and caprichos. by jerome rothenberg

eye of witness: a jerome rothenberg reader. edited by heriberto yepez and jerome rothenberg

soraya. by anis shivani

fractal song. by jerry w. ward, jr.

beginnings of the prose poem. edited by mary ann caws and michel delville

black widow press poetry in translation

the great madness. by avigdor hameiri. translated and edited by peter c. appelbaum.

of human carnage - odessa 1918-1920. by avigdor hameiri. translated and edited by peter c. appelbaum. introduction by dan hecht

howls & growls: french poems to bark by. translated by norman r. shapiro & illustrated by olga pastuchiv

a flea the size of paris: the old french "fatrasies" and "fatras". translated by ted byrne and donato mancini

in praise of sleep: selected poems of lucian blaga. by lucian blaga. translated by andrei codrescu

rhymamusings. by pierre coran. translated by norman r. shapiro

through naked branches: selected poems of tarjei vesaas. by tarjei vesaas. translated by roger greenwald

i have invented nothing: selected poems. by jean-pierre rosnay. translated by j. kates

fables of town & country. by pierre coran. translated by norman r. shapiro & illustrated by olga pastuchiv

earthlight (clair de terre): poems. by andré breton. translated by bill zavatsky and zack rogow

the gentle genius of cecile perin: selected poems (1906-1956). by cecile perin. translated by norman r. shapiro *boris vian invents boris vian: a boris vian reader.* by boris vian. edited and translated by julia older with a preface by patrick vian

forbidden pleasures: new selected poems [1924-1949]. by luis cernuda. translated by stephen kessler

fables in a modern key (fables dans l'air du temps). by pierre coran. translated by norman r. shapiro & illustrated by olga pastuchiv

exile is my trade: a habib tengour reader. by habib tengour. translated by pierre joris

present tense of the world: poems 2000-2009. by amina said. translated by marilyn hacker

endure: poems. by bei dao. translated by clayton eshleman and lucas klein

curdled skulls: poems of bernard bador. by bernard bador. co-translated and edited by clayton eshleman

pierre reverdy: poems early to late. by pierre reverdy. translated by mary ann caws and patricia terry

selected prose and poetry of jules supervielle. by jules supervielle. translated by nancy kline, patrica terry, and kathleen micklow

poems of consummation. by vicente aleixandre. translated by stephen kessler

a life of poems, poems of a life. by anna de noailles. translated by norman r. shapiro

furor & mystery and other poems. by rene char. translated by mary ann caws and nancy kline

the big game (le grand jeu). by benjamin péret. translated by marilyn kallet

essential poems & prose of jules laforgue. by jules laforgue. translated by patricia terry

preversities: a jacques prevert sampler. by jacques prevert. translated by norman r. shapiro

la fontaine's bawdy. by jean de la fontaine. translated by norman r. shapiro & illustrated by david schorr

inventor of love. by gherasim luca. translated by julian and laura semilian

art poetique. by guillevic. translated by maureen smith with lucie albertini guillevic

to speak, to tell you? by sabine sicaud. translated by norman r. shapiro

poems of a. o. barnabooth. by valery larbaud. translated by ron padgett and bill zavatsky

eyeseas (les ziaux). by raymond queneau. translated by daniela hurezanu and stephen kessler

essential poems and writings of joyce mansour. by joyce mansour. translated by serge gavronsky *essential poems and writings of robert desnos: a bilingual anthology.* by robert desnos. translated by mary ann caws, terry hale, bill zavatsky, martin sorrell, jonathan eburne, katherine connelly, patricia terry, and paul auster

the sea and other poems (1977-1997). by guillevic. translated by patricia terry

love, poetry, (l'amour la poesie, 1929). by paul eluard. translated by stuart kendall

capital of pain. by paul eluard. translated by mary ann caws, patricia terry, and nancy kline

poems of andré breton, a bilingual anthology. by andré breton. translated by jean-pierre cauvin and mary ann caws

last love poems of paul eluard. by paul eluard. translated by marilyn kallet

approximate man' & other writings. by tristan tzara. translated by mary ann caws

chanson dada: selected poems of tristan tzara. by tristan tzara. translated by lee harwood

disenchanted city: la ville désenchantée. by chantel bizzini. translated by marilyn kallet and j. bradford anderson

guarding the air: selected poems of gunnar harding. by gunnar harding. translated by roger greenwald

black widow press biography

revolution of the mind: the life of andre breton. by mark polizzotti

www.blackwidowpress.com